*Occult Symbolism
of the Sun and Moon,
the Goddess Isis
and the Solar Deities*

By
Manly P. Hall

Copyright © 2022 Lamp of Trismegistus. All rights reserved. No part of this publication may be reproduced or transmitted in any form or by any means, electronic or mechanical, including photocopying, recording, or by any information storage and retrieval system, without permission in writing from Lamp of Trismegistus. Reviewers may quote brief passages.

ISBN: 978-1-63118-611-0

*Esoteric Classics*

## Other Books in this Series and Related Titles

*Aurora of the Philosophers* by Paracelsus (978-1-63118-507-6)

*Rosicrucian Rules, Secret Signs, Codes and Symbols* by various (978-1-63118-488-8)

*On the Philadelphian Gold* by Philochrysus & Philadelphus (978-1-63118-511-3)

*Paracelsus, the Four Elements and Their Spirits* by M P Hall (978-1-63118-400-0)

*The Stone of the Philosophers* by A E Waite (978-1-63118-509-0)

*Clairvoyance and Psychic Abilities* by A Besant &c (978-1-63118-403-1)

*The Rosicrucian Chemical Marriage* by Christian Rosenkreuz (978-1-63118-458-1)

*The Alchemical Catechism of Paracelsus* by Paracelsus (978-1-63118-513-7)

*Alchemy in the Nineteenth Century* by Helena P. Blavatsky (978-1-63118-446-8)

*Rosicrucians and Speculative Masonry in the Seventeenth Century* (978-1-63118-489-5)

*Qabbalistic Teachings and the Tree of Life* by M P Hall (978-1-63118-482-6)

*The Sepher Yetzirah and the Qabalah* by M P Hall (978-1-63118-481-9)

*The Devil in Love* by Jacques Cazotte (978–1–63118–499–4)

*Fortune-Telling with Dice* by Astra Cielo (978-1-63118-466-6)

*History, Analysis and Secret Tradition of the Tarot* by Hall &c (978-1-63118-445-1)

*Crystal Vision Through Crystal Gazing* by Frater Achad (978-1-63118-455-0)

*The Golden Verses of Pythagoras: Five Translations* (978-1-63118-479-6)

*Arcane Formulas or Mental Alchemy* by W W Atkinson (978-1-63118-459-8)

*The Machinery of the Mind* by Dion Fortune (978-1-63118-451-2)

*The A E Waite Reader: A Selection of Occult Essays* (978-1-63118-515-1)

*The Leadbeater Reader: A Selection of Occult Essays* (978-1-63118-483-3)

**Audio versions are also available on Audible, Amazon and Apple**

## Other Books in this Series and Related Titles

*Practical Theosophy* by Annie Besant (978–1–63118–610–3)

*The Human Body in Symbolism* by Manly P Hall (978–1–63118–609–7)

*Theosophical Basics* by William Q Judge (978–1–63118–608–0)

*The Hebrew Talisman* by Richard Harte (978–1–63118–607–3)

*Early Masonic Symbolism* by Manly P Hall (978–1–63118–606–6)

*Nature Spirits and Elementals* by Louise Off (978-1-63118-605-9)

*Swedenborg Bifrons* by H P Blavatsky (978-1-63118-604-2)

*Practical Use of Psychic Powers* by C W Leadbeater (978-1-63118-603-5)

*Using White & Black Magic* by C W Leadbeater (978-1-63118-602-8)

*Jesus, the Last Great Initiate* by Edouard Schure (978-1-63118-599-1)

*Mysterious Wonders of Antiquity* by Manly P Hall (978-1-63118-598-4)

*Ancient Mysteries and Secret Societies* by Manly P Hall (978–1–63118–597–7)

*The Zodiac and Its Signs* by Manly P Hall (978–1–63118–596–0)

*Life and Teachings of Hermes Trismegistus* by Manly P Hall (978–1–63118–595–3)

*The Secrets of Doctor Taverner* by Dion Fortune (978–1–63118–594–6)

*Vegetarianism, Theosophy & Occultism* by Leadbeater &c (978–1–63118–593–9)

*Applied Theosophy* by Henry S Olcott (978–1–63118–592–2)

*Higher Consciousness* by C W Leadbeater (978–1–63118–591–5)

*Theories About Reincarnation and Spirits* by H P Blavatsky (978–1–63118–590–8)

*The Use and Power of Thought* by C W Leadbeater (978–1–63118–589–2)

*Commentary on the Pymander* by G R S Mead (978–1–63118–588–5)

**Audio versions are also available on Audible, Amazon and Apple**

# Table of Contents

Introduction...7

*The Virgin of the World*...9

*Mummification of the Egyptian Dead*...26

*The Universal Deity*...29

*The Solar Trinity*...31

*Christianity and the Sun*...36

*The Birthday of the Sun*...38

*The Three Suns*...41

*The Celestial Inhabitants of the Sun*...44

*The Sun in Alchemical Symbology*...46

*The Midnight Sun*...48

*Solar Colors*...50

# INTRODUCTION

The word "esoteric" can be difficult to define. Esotericism in general can be seen less as a system of beliefs and more as a category, which encompasses numerous, different systems of beliefs. It's a bit of juxtaposition, since the word "esoteric" indicates something that few people know about, while the term itself broadly covers numerous philosophies, practices, areas of study and belief systems.

In a greater sense, Esotericism acts as a storehouse for secret knowledge, which is often considered ancient (by *tradition, if not by fact*), passed down from generation to generation, in private. At various times in history, simply possessing the knowledge of some of these subjects, was considered illegal and a jailable offence, if discovered. This usually included such general topics as Alchemy, Pharmacology, Qabalah, Hermeticism, Occultism, Ceremonial Magic, Astrology, Divination, Rosicrucianism and so on. Collectively, these areas of study were often referred to as the esoteric sciences.

Sometimes, the outer garment of a subject isn't esoteric, while what is hidden beneath it, is. As an example, Freemasonry isn't necessarily esoteric by nature (at *least not anymore),* but certain signs, passwords and handshakes given to the candidate during their initiation, are in fact, esoteric, in the sense that they are hidden from the general public.

Today, in the twenty-first century, such topics are readily available at bookstores across the country, and numerous main-steam publishers offer beginners guides and coffee-table volumes on many of these subjects, intended for mass appeal. Books like *"The Secret"* have turned previously arcane topics into household knowledge. All that being the case, however, it isn't to say that there still aren't buried secrets to uncover, ancient wisdom being ignored and forgotten mysteries to be explored. In fact, it is often that we are only able to further our own studies by standing on the shoulders of these disappearing giants.

Lamp of Trismegistus is doing its part to help preserve humanity's esoteric history by making some of these classics available to those students who are seeking to unearth the knowledge of these ancient colossi.

So, be sure to check other titles from our *Esoteric Classics* series, as well as our *Occult Fiction, Theosophical Classics, Foundations of Freemasonry Series, Supernatural Fiction, Paranormal Research Series, Studies in Buddhism* and our *Christian Apocrypha Series.* You can also download the audio versions of most of these titles from Amazon, Apple or Audible, for learning on the go.

# PART I:
# The Virgin of the World

It is especially fitting that a study of Hermetic symbolism should begin with a discussion of the symbols and attributes of the *Saitic Isis*. This is the Isis of Sais, famous for the inscription concerning her which appeared on the front of her temple in that city: "*I, Isis, am all that has been, that is or shall be; no mortal Man hath ever me unveiled.*"

Plutarch affirms that many ancient authors believed this goddess to be the daughter of Hermes; others held the opinion that she was the child of Prometheus. Both of these demigods were noted for their divine wisdom. It is not improbable that her kinship to them is merely allegorical. Plutarch translates the name Isis to mean wisdom. Godfrey Higgins, in his *Anacalypsis*, derives the name of Isis from the Hebrew name "*Iso*," and the Greek word meaning "to save." Some authorities, however, for example, Richard Payne Knight, as stated in his book, *Symbolical Language of Ancient Art and Mythology*, believe the word to be of Northern extraction, possibly Scandinavian or Gothic. In these languages the name is pronounced *Isa*, meaning *ice*, or water in its most passive, crystallized, negative state.

This Egyptian deity under many names appears as the principle of natural fecundity among nearly all the religions of the ancient world. She was known as the goddess with ten thousand appellations and was metamorphosed by Christianity into the Virgin Mary, for Isis, although she gave birth to all living things--chief among them the Sun--still remained a virgin, according to the legendary accounts.

Apuleius in the eleventh book of *The Golden Ass* ascribes to the goddess the following statement concerning her powers and attributes:

> "Behold, I, moved by thy prayers, am present with thee; I, who am Nature, the parent of things, the queen of all the elements, the primordial progeny of ages, the supreme of Divinities, the sovereign of the spirits of the dead, the first of the celestials, and the uniform resemblance of Gods and Goddesses. I, who rule by my nod the luminous summits of the heavens, the salubrious breezes of the sea, and the deplorable silences of the

realms beneath, and whose one divinity the whole orb of the earth venerates under a manifold form, by different rites and a variety of appellations. Hence the primogenial Phrygians call me Pessinuntica, the mother of the Gods, the Attic Aborigines, Cecropian Minerva; the floating Cyprians, Paphian Venus; the arrow-bearing Cretans, Diana Dictynna; the three-tongued Sicilians, Stygian Proserpine; and the Eleusinians, the ancient Goddess Ceres. Some also call me Juno, others Bellona, others Hecate, and others Rhamnusia. And those who are illuminated by the incipient rays of that divinity the Sun, when he rises, viz. the Ethiopians, the Arii, and the Egyptians skilled in ancient learning, worshipping me by ceremonies perfectly appropriate, call me by my true name, Queen Isis."

Augustus Le Plongeon believed that the Egyptian myth of Isis had a historical basis among the Mayas of Central America, where this goddess was known as Queen Moo. In Prince Coh the same author finds a correspondence to Osiris, the brother-husband of Isis. Le Plongeon's theory is that Mayan civilization was far more ancient than that of Egypt. After the death of Prince Coh, his widow, Queen Moo, fleeing to escape the wrath of his murderers, sought refuge among the Mayan colonies in Egypt, where she was accepted as their queen and was given the name of Isis. While Le Plongeon may be right, the possible historical queen sinks into insignificance when compared with the allegorical, symbolic World Virgin; and the fact that she appears among so many different races and peoples discredits the theory that she was a historical individual.

According to Sextus Empyricus, the Trojan war was fought over a statue of the moon goddess. For this lunar Helena, and not for a woman, the Greeks and Trojans struggled at the gates of Troy.

Several authors have attempted to prove that Isis, Osiris, Typhon, Nephthys, and Aroueris (*Thoth, or Mercury*) were grandchildren of the great Jewish patriarch Noah by his son Ham. But as the story of Noah and his ark is a cosmic allegory concerning the repopulation of planets at the beginning of each world period, this only makes it less likely that they were historical personages. According to Robert Fludd, the sun has three properties--*life*, *light*, and *heat*. These three vivify and vitalize the three worlds--spiritual, intellectual, and material. Therefore, it is said *"from one light, three lights,"* i.e. the first three Master Masons. In all probability, Osiris represents the third, or material, aspect of solar activity, which by its beneficent influences vitalizes and enlivens the flora and fauna of the earth. Osiris is not the sun, but the sun is symbolic of the vital principle of Nature, which the ancients knew as Osiris. His symbol, therefore, was an opened eye, in honor of the Great Eye of the universe, the sun. Opposed to the active, radiant principle of impregnating fire, hear, and motion was the passive, receptive principle of Nature.

Modern science has proved that forms ranging in magnitude from solar systems to atoms are composed of positive, radiant nuclei surrounded by negative bodies that exist upon the emanations of the central life. From this allegory we have the story of Solomon and his wives, for Solomon is the sun and his wives and concubines are the planets, moons, asteroids, and other receptive bodies within his house-- the solar mansion. Isis, represented in the *Song of Solomon* by the dark maid of Jerusalem, is symbolic of receptive Nature--the watery, maternal principle which creates all things out of herself after impregnation has been achieved by the virility of the sun.

In the ancient world the year had 360 days. The five extra days were gathered together by the God of Cosmic Intelligence to serve as the birthdays of the five gods and goddesses who are called the sons and daughters of Ham. Upon the first of these special days Osiris was born and upon the fourth of them Isis (the number *four* shows the relation that this goddess bears to the earth and its elements.) Typhon, the Egyptian Demon or Spirit of the Adversary, was born upon the third day. Typhon is often symbolized by a crocodile; sometimes his body is a combination of crocodile and hog. Isis stands for knowledge and wisdom, and according to Plutarch the word *Typhon* means insolence and pride. Egotism, self-centeredness, and pride are the deadly enemies of understanding and truth. This part of the allegory is revealed.

After Osiris, here symbolized as the sun, had become King of Egypt and had given to his people the full advantage of his intellectual light, he continued his path through the heavens, visiting the peoples of other nations and converting all with whom he came in contact. Plutarch further asserts that the Greeks recognized in Osiris the same person whom they revered under the names of *Dionysos* and *Bacchus*. While he was away from his country, his brother, Typhon, the Evil One, like the Loki of

ISIS, QUEEN OF HEAVEN[1]

---

[1] From Mosaize *Historie der Hebreeuwse Kerke*.

Diodorus writes of a famous inscription carved on a column at Nysa, in Arabia, wherein Isis described herself as follows: "I am Isis, Queen of this country. I was instructed by Mercury. No one can destroy the laws which I have established. I am the eldest daughter of Saturn, most ancient of the gods. I am the wife and sister of Osiris the King. I first made known to mortals the use of wheat. I am the mother of Orus the King. In my honor was the city of Bubaste built. Rejoice, O Egypt, rejoice, land that gave me birth!" (See "Morals and Dogma," by Albert Pike.)

Scandinavia, plotted against the Sun God to destroy him. Gathering seventy-two persons as fellow conspirators, he attained his nefarious end in a most subtle manner. He had a wonderful ornamented box made just the size of the body of Osiris. This he brought into a banquet hall where the gods and goddesses were feasting together. All admired the beautiful chest, and Typhon promised to give it to the one whose body fitted it most perfectly. One after another lay down in the box, but in disappointment rose again, until at last Osiris also tried. The moment he was in the chest Typhon and his accomplices nailed the cover down and sealed the cracks with molten lead. They then cast the box into the Nile, down which it floated to the sea. Plutarch states that the date upon which this occurred was the seventeenth day of the month Athyr, when the sun was in the constellation of Scorpio. This is most significant, for the Scorpion is the symbol of treachery. The time when Osiris entered the chest was also the same season that Noah entered the ark to escape from the Deluge.

Plutarch further declares that the Pans and Satyrs (the Nature spirits and elementals) first discovered that Osiris had been murdered. These immediately raised an alarm, and from this incident the word panic, meaning *fright* or amazement of the multitudes, originated. Isis, upon receiving the news of her husband's murder, which she learned from some children who had seen the murderers making off with the box, at once robed herself in mourning and started forth in quest of him.

At length Isis discovered that the chest had floated to the coast of Byblos. There it had lodged in the branches of a tree, which in a short time miraculously grew up around the box. This so amazed the king of that country that he ordered the tree to be cut down and a pillar made from its trunk to support the roof of his palace. Isis, visiting Byblos, recovered the body of her husband, but it was again stolen by Typhon, who cut it into fourteen parts, which he scattered all over the earth. Isis, in despair, began gathering up the severed remains of her husband, but found only thirteen pieces. The fourteenth part *(the phallus)* she reproduced in gold, for the original had fallen into the river Nile and had been swallowed by a fish.

Typhon was later slain in battle by the son of Osiris. Some of the Egyptians believed that the souls of the gods were taken to heaven, where they shone forth as stars. It was supposed that the soul of Isis gleamed from the Dog Star, while Typhon became the constellation of the Bear. It is doubtful, however, whether this idea was ever generally accepted.

Among the Egyptians, Isis is often represented with a headdress consisting of the empty throne chair of her murdered husband, and this peculiar structure was accepted during certain dynasties as her hieroglyphic. The headdresses of the Egyptians have great symbolic and emblematic importance, for they represent the auric bodies of the superhuman intelligences, and are used in the same way that the nimbus, halo, and aureole are used in Christian religious art. Frank C. Higgins, a well-known Masonic symbolist, has astutely noted that the ornate headgears of certain gods and Pharaohs are inclined backward at the same angle as the earth's axis. The robes, insignia, jewels, and ornamentations of the ancient hierophants symbolized the spiritual energies radiating from the human body. Modern science is rediscovering many of the lost secrets of Hermetic philosophy. One of these is the ability to gauge the mental development, the soul qualities, and the physical health of an individual from the streamers of semi-visible electric force which pour through the surface of the skin of every human being at all times during his life.

Isis is sometimes symbolized by the head of a cow; occasionally the entire animal is her symbol. The first gods of the Scandinavians were licked out of blocks of ice by the Mother Cow, *Audhumla*, who symbolized the principle of natural nutriment and fecundity because of her milk. Occasionally Isis is represented as a bird. She often carries in one hand the *crux ansata*, the symbol of eternal life, and in the other the flowered scepter, symbolic of her authority.

Thoth Hermes Trismegistus, the founder of Egyptian learning, the Wise Man of the ancient world, gave to the priests and philosophers of antiquity the secrets which have been preserved to this day in myth and legend. These allegories and emblematic figures conceal the secret formula for spiritual, mental, moral, and physical regeneration commonly known as the Mystic Chemistry of the Soul (i.e. alchemy). These sublime truths were communicated to the initiates of the Mystery Schools, but were concealed from the profane. The latter, unable to understand the abstract philosophical tenets, worshiped the concrete sculptured idols which were emblematic of these secret truths. The wisdom and secrecy of Egypt are epitomized in the Sphinx, which has preserved its secret from the seekers of a hundred generations. The mysteries of Hermeticism, the great spiritual truths hidden from the world by the ignorance of the world, and the keys of the secret doctrines of the ancient philosophers, are all symbolized by the Virgin Isis. Veiled from head to foot, she reveals her wisdom only to the tried and initiated few who have earned the right to enter her sacred presence, tear from the veiled figure of Nature its shroud of obscurity, and stand face to face with the Divine Reality.

The explanations in these pages of the symbols peculiar to the Virgin Isis are based (unless otherwise noted) on selections from a translation of the fourth book of *Bibliotèque des Philosophes Hermétiques*, entitled "The Hermetical Signification of the Symbols and Attributes of Isis," with interpolations by the compiler to amplify and clarify the text.

The statues of Isis were decorated with the sun, moon, and stars, and many emblems pertaining to the earth, over which Isis was believed to rule (as the guardian spirit of Nature personified). Several images of the goddess have been found upon which the marks of her dignity and position were still intact. According to the ancient philosophers, she personified Universal Nature, the mother of all productions. The deity was generally represented as a partly nude woman, often pregnant, sometimes loosely covered with a garment either of green or black color, or of four different shades intermingled: black, white, yellow, and red.

Apuleius describes her as follows:

> "In the first place, then, her most copious and long hairs, being gradually intorted, and promiscuously scattered on her divine neck, were softly defluous. A multiform crown, consisting of various flowers, bound the sublime summit of her head. And in the middle of the crown, just on her forehead, there was a smooth orb resembling a mirror, or rather a white refulgent light, which indicated that she was the moon. Vipers rising up after the manner of furrows, environed the crown on the right hand and

on the left, and Cerealian ears of corn were also extended from above. Her garment was of many colours, and woven from the finest flax, and was at one time lucid with a white splendour, at another yellow from the flower of crocus, and at another flaming with a rosy redness. But that which most excessively dazzled my sight, was a very black robe, fulgid with a dark splendour, and which, spreading round and passing under her right side, and ascending to her left shoulder, there rose protuberant like the center of a shield, the dependent part of the robe falling in many folds, and having small knots of fringe, gracefully flowing in its extremities. Glittering stars were dispersed through the embroidered border of the robe, and through the whole of its surface: and the full moon, shining in the middle of the stars, breathed forth flaming fires. Nevertheless, a crown, wholly consisting of flowers and fruits of every kind, adhered with indivisible connection to the border of that conspicuous robe, in all its undulating motions. What she carried in her hands also consisted of things of a very different nature. For her right hand, indeed, bore a brazen rattle (*sistrum*) through the narrow lamina of which bent like a belt, certain rods passing, produced a sharp triple sound, through the vibrating motion of her arm. An oblong vessel, in the shape of a boat, depended from her left hand, on the handle of which, in that part in which it was conspicuous, an asp raised its erect head and largely swelling neck. And shoes woven from the leaves of the victorious palm tree covered her immortal feet."

The green color alludes to the vegetation which covers the face of the earth, and therefore represents the robe of Nature. The black represents death and corruption as being the way to a new life and generation. "Except a man be born again, he cannot see the kingdom of God." (John iii. 3.) White, yellow, and red signify the three principal colors of the alchemical, Hermetical, universal medicine after the blackness of its putrefaction is over.

The ancients gave the name Isis to one of their occult medicines; therefore, the description here given relates somewhat to chemistry. Her black drape also signifies that the moon, or the lunar humidity--the sophic universal mercury and the operating substance of Nature in alchemical terminology--has no light of its own, but receives its light, its fire, and its vitalizing force from the sun. Isis was the image or representative of the Great Works of the wise men: the Philosopher's Stone, the Elixir of Life, and the Universal Medicine.

THE SISTRUM[2]

---

[2] "The sistrum is designed * * * to represent to us, that every thing must be kept in continual agitation, and never cease from motion; that they ought to be mused and well-shaken, whenever they begin to grow drowsy as it were, and to droop in their motion. For, say they, the sound of these sistra averts and drives away Typho; meaning hereby, that as corruption clogs and puts a stop to the regular course of nature; so generation, by the means of motion, loosens it again, and restores it to its former vigour. Now the outer surface of this instrument is of a convex figure, as within its circumference are contained those four chords or bars [only three shown], which make such a rattling when they are shaken--nor is this without its meaning; for that part of the universe which is subject to generation and corruption is contained within the sphere of the moon; and whatever motions or changes may happen therein, they are all effected by the different combinations of the four elementary bodies, fire, earth, water, and air--moreover, upon the upper part of the convex surface of the sistrum is carved the effigies of a cat with a human visage, as on the lower edge of it,

Other hieroglyphics seen in connection with Isis are no less curious than those already described, but it is impossible to enumerate all, for many symbols were used interchangeably by the Egyptian Hermetists. The goddess often wore upon her head a hat made of cypress branches, to signify mourning for her dead husband and also for the physical death which she caused every creature to undergo in order to receive a new life in posterity or a periodic resurrection. The head of Isis is sometimes ornamented with a crown of gold or a garland of olive leaves, as conspicuous marks of her sovereignty as queen of the world and mistress of the entire universe. The crown of gold signifies also the aurific unctuosity or sulphurous fatness of the solar and vital fires which she dispenses to every individual by a continual circulation of the elements, this circulation being symbolized by the musical rattle which she carries in her hand. This sistrum is also the yonic symbol of purity.

A serpent interwoven among the olive leaves on her head, devouring its own tail, denotes that the aurific unctuosity was soiled with the venom of terrestrial corruption which surrounded it and must be mortified and purified by seven planetary circulations or purifications called *flying eagles* (alchemical terminology) in order to make it medicinal for the restoration of health. (Here the emanations from the sun are recognized as a medicine for the healing of human ills.) The seven planetary circulations are represented by the circumambulations of the Masonic lodge; by the marching of the Jewish priests seven times around the walls of Jericho, and of the Mohammedan priests seven times around the Kabba at Mecca. From the crown of gold project three horns of plenty, signifying the abundance of the gifts of Nature proceeding from one root having its origin in the heavens (head of Isis).

---

under those moving chords, is engraved on the one side the face of Isis, and on the other that of Nephthys--by the faces symbolically representing generation and corruption (which, as has been already observed, is nothing but the motion and alteration of the four elements one amongst another),"

(From Plutarch's *Isis and Osiris*.)

In this figure the pagan naturalists represent all the vital powers of the three kingdoms and families of sublunary nature: mineral, plant, and animal (man being considered as an animal). At one of her ears was the moon and at the other the sun, to indicate that these two were the agent and patient, or father and mother principles of all natural objects; and that Isis, or Nature, makes use of these two luminaries to communicate her powers to the whole empire of animals, vegetables, and minerals. On the back of her neck were the characters of the planets and the signs of the zodiac which assisted the planets in their functions. This signified that the heavenly influences directed the destinies of the principles and sperms of all things, because they were the governors of all sublunary bodies, which they transformed into little worlds made in the image of the greater universe.

Isis holds in her right hand a small sailing ship with the spindle of a spinning wheel for its mast. From the top of the mast projects a water jug, its handle shaped like a serpent swelled with venom. This indicates that Isis steers the bark of life, full of troubles and miseries, on the stormy ocean of Time. The spindle symbolizes the fact that she spins and cuts the thread of Life. These emblems further signify that Isis abounds in humidity, by means of which she nourishes all natural bodies, preserving them from the heat of the sun by humidifying them with nutritious moisture from the atmosphere. Moisture supports vegetation, but this subtle humidity (life's ether) is always more or less infected by some venom proceeding from corruption or decay. It must be purified by being brought into contact with the invisible cleansing fire of Nature. This fire digests, perfects, and revitalizes this substance, in order that the humidity may become a universal medicine to heal and renew all the bodies in Nature.

The serpent throws off its skin annually and is thereby renewed (symbolic of the resurrection of the spiritual life from the material nature). This renewal of the earth takes place every spring, when the vivifying spirit of the sun returns to the countries of the Northern Hemisphere,

The symbolic Virgin carries in her left hand a sistrum and a cymbal, or square frame of metal, which when struck gives the key-note of Nature (Fa); sometimes also an olive branch, to indicate the harmony she preserves among natural things with her regenerating power. By the processes of death and corruption she gives life to a number of creatures of diverse forms through periods of perpetual change. The cymbal is made square instead of the usual triangular shape in order to symbolize that all things are transmuted and regenerated according to the harmony of the four elements.

Dr. Sigismund Bacstrom believed that if a physician could establish harmony among the elements of earth, fire, air, and water, and unite them into a stone (the Philosopher's Stone) symbolized by the six-pointed star or two interlaced triangles, he would possess the means of healing all disease. Dr. Bacstrom further stated that there was no doubt in his mind that the universal, omnipresent fire (spirit) of Nature: "does all and is all in all." By attraction, repulsion, motion, heat, sublimation, evaporation, exsiccation, inspissation, coagulation, and fixation, the Universal Fire (Spirit) manipulates matter, and manifests throughout creation. Any individual who can understand these principles and adapt them to the three departments of Nature becomes a true philosopher.

From the right breast of Isis protruded a bunch of grapes and from the left an ear of corn or a sheaf of wheat, golden in color. These indicate that Nature is the source of nutrition for plant, animal, and human life, nourishing all things from herself. The golden color in the wheat (corn) indicates that in the sunlight or spiritual gold is concealed the first sperm of all life.

On the girdle surrounding the upper part of the body of the statue appear a number of mysterious emblems. The girdle is joined together in front by four golden plates (the elements), placed in the form of a square. This signified that Isis, or Nature, the first matter (alchemical terminology), was the essence- of the four elements (life, light, heat, and force), which quintessence generated all things. Numerous stars are represented on this girdle, thereby indicating their influence in darkness as well as the influence of the sun in light. Isis is the Virgin immortalized in the constellation of Virgo, where the World Mother is placed with the serpent under her feet and a crown. of stars on her head. In her arms she carries a sheaf of grain and sometimes the young Sun God.

The statue of Isis was placed on a pedestal of dark stone ornamented with rams' heads. Her feet trod upon a number of venomous reptiles. This indicates that Nature has power to free from acidity or saltness all corrosives and to overcome all impurities from terrestrial corruption adhering to bodies. The rams' heads indicate that the most auspicious time for the generation of life is during the period when the sun passes through the sign of Aries. The serpents under her feet indicate that Nature is inclined to preserve life and to heal disease by expelling impurities and corruption.

In this sense the axioms known to the ancient philosophers are verified; namely:

*Nature contains Nature,*
*Nature rejoices in her own nature,*
*Nature surmounts Nature;*
*Nature cannot be amended but in her own nature.*

Therefore, in contemplating the statue of Isis, we must not lose sight of the occult sense of its allegories; otherwise, the Virgin remains an inexplicable enigma.

From a golden ring on her left arm a line descends, to the end of which is suspended a deep box filled with flaming coals and incense. Isis, or Nature personified, carries with her the sacred fire, religiously preserved and kept burning in a special temple by the vestal virgins. This fire is the genuine, immortal flame of Nature--ethereal, essential, the author of life. The inconsumable oil; the balsam of life, so much praised by the wise and so often referred to in the Scriptures, is frequently symbolized as the fuel of this immortal flame.

From the right arm of the figure also descends a thread, to the end of which is fastened a pair of scales, to denote the exactitude of Nature in her weights and measures. Isis is often represented as the symbol of justice, because Nature is eternally consistent.

The World Virgin is sometimes shown standing between two great pillars--the Jachin and Boaz of Freemasonry--symbolizing the fact that Nature attains productivity by means of polarity. As wisdom personified, Isis stands between the pillars of opposites, demonstrating that understanding is always found at the point of equilibrium and that truth is often crucified between the two thieves of apparent contradiction.

THOTH, THE DOG-HEADED[3]

The sheen of gold in her dark hair indicates that while she is lunar, her power is due to the sun's rays, from which she secures her ruddy complexion. As the moon is robed in the reflected light of the sun, so Isis, like the virgin of Revelation, is clothed in the glory of solar luminosity. Apuleius states that while he was sleeping he beheld the venerable goddess Isis rising out of the ocean. The ancients realized that the primary forms of life first came out of water, and modem science concurs in this view. H. G. Wells, in his *Outline of History*, describing primitive life on the earth,

---

[3] From Lenoir's *La Franche-Maconnerie*.
Aroueris, or Thoth, one of the five immortals, protected the infant Horus from the wrath of Typhon after the murder of Osiris. He also revised the ancient Egyptian calendar by increasing the year from 360 days to 365. Thoth Hermes was called "The Dog-Headed" because of his faithfulness and integrity. He is shown crowned with a solar nimbus, carrying in one hand the Crux Ansata, the symbol of eternal life, and in the other a serpent-wound staff symbolic of his dignity as counselor of the gods.

states: "But though the ocean and intertidal water already swarmed with life, the land above the high-tide line was still, so far as we can guess, a

THE EGYPTIAN MADONNA[4]

stony wilderness without a trace of life." In the next chapter he adds: "Wherever the shore-line ran there was life, and that life went on in and by and with water as its home, its medium, and its fundamental necessity." The ancients believed that the universal sperm proceeded from warm vapor, humid but fiery. The veiled Isis, whose very coverings represent vapor, is symbolic of this humidity, which is the carrier or vehicle for the sperm life of the sun, represented by a child in her arms. Because the sun, moon, and stars in setting appear to sink into the sea and also because the

---

[4] From Lenoir's *La Franche-Maconnerie*.

Isis is shown with her son Horus in her arms. She is crowned with the lunar orb, ornamented with the horns of rams or bulls. Orus, or Horus as he is more generally known, was the son of Isis and Osiris. He was the god of time, hours, days, and this narrow span of life recognized as mortal existence. In all probability, the four sons of Horus represent the four kingdoms of Nature. It was Horus who finally avenged the murder of his father, Osiris, by slaying Typhon, the spirit of Evil.

water receives their rays into itself, the sea was believed to be the breeding ground for the sperm of living things. This sperm is generated from the combination of the influences of the celestial bodies; hence Isis is sometimes represented as pregnant.

Frequently the statue of Isis was accompanied by the figure of a large black and white ox. The ox represents either Osiris as Taurus, the bull of the zodiac, or Apis, an animal sacred to Osiris because of its peculiar markings and colorings. Among the Egyptians, the bull was a beast of burden. Hence the presence of the animal was a reminder of the labors patiently performed by Nature that all creatures may have life and health. Harpocrates, the God of Silence, holding his fingers to his mouth, often accompanies the statue of Isis. He warns all to keep the secrets of the wise from those unfit to know them.

The Druids of Britain and Gaul had a deep knowledge concerning the mysteries of Isis and worshiped her under the symbol of the moon. Godfrey Higgins considers it a mistake to regard Isis as synonymous with the moon. The moon was chosen for Isis because of its dominion over water. The Druids considered the sun to be the father and the moon the mother of all things. By means of these symbols they worshiped Universal Nature.

The figure of Isis is sometimes used to represent the occult and magical arts, such as necromancy, invocation, sorcery, and thaumaturgy. In one of the myths concerning her, Isis is said to have conjured the invincible God of Eternities, *Ra*, to tell her his secret and sacred name, which he did. This name is equivalent to the Lost Word of Masonry. By means of this Word, a magician can demand obedience from the invisible and superior deities. The priests of Isis became adepts in the use of the unseen forces of Nature. They understood hypnotism, mesmerism, and similar practices long before the modem world dreamed of their existence.

Plutarch describes the requisites of a follower of Isis in this manner: "For as 'tis not the length of the beard, or the coarseness of the habit which makes a philosopher, so neither will those frequent shavings, or the mere wearing of a linen vestment constitute a votary of Isis; but he alone is a true servant or follower of this Goddess, who after he has heard, and been made acquainted in a proper manner with the history of the actions of these Gods, searches into the hidden truths which he concealed under them, and examines the whole by the dictates of reason and philosophy."

During the Middle Ages the troubadours of Central Europe preserved in song the legends of this Egyptian goddess. They composed sonnets to the most beautiful woman in all the world. Though few ever discovered her identity, she was Sophia, the Virgin of Wisdom, whom all the philosophers of the world have wooed. Isis represents the mystery of motherhood, which the ancients recognized as the most apparent proof of Nature's omniscient wiscom and God's overshadowing power. To the modern seeker she is the epitome of the Great Unknown, and only those who unveil her will be able to solve the mysteries of life, death, generation, and regeneration.

# PART II:
# Mummification of the Egyptian Dead

Servius, commenting on Virgil's *Æneid*, observes that "the wise Egyptians took care to embalm their bodies, and deposit them in catacombs, in order that the soul might be preserved for a long time in connection with the body, and might not soon be alienated; while the Romans, with an opposite design, committed the remains of their dead to the funeral pile, intending that the vital spark might immediately be restored to the general element, or return to its pristine nature."

No complete records are available which give the secret doctrine of the Egyptians concerning the relationship existing between the spirit, or consciousness, and the body which it inhabited. It is reasonably certain, however, that Pythagoras, who had been initiated in the Egyptian temples, when he promulgated the doctrine of metempsychosis, restated, in part at least, the teachings of the Egyptian initiates. The popular supposition that the Egyptians mummified their dead in order to preserve the form for a physical resurrection is untenable in the light of modern knowledge regarding their philosophy of death. In the fourth book of *On Abstinence from Animal Food*, Porphyry describes an Egyptian custom of purifying the dead by removing the contents of the abdominal cavity, which they placed in a separate chest. He then reproduces the following oration which had been translated out of the Egyptian tongue by Euphantus: "O sovereign Sun, and all ye Gods who impart life to men, receive me, and deliver me to the eternal Gods as a cohabitant. For I have always piously worshipped those divinities which were pointed out to me by my parents as long as I lived in this age, and have likewise always honored those who procreated my body. And, with respect to other men, I have never slain any one, nor defrauded any one of what he deposited with me, nor have I committed any other atrocious deed. If, therefore, during my life I have acted erroneously, by eating or drinking things which it is unlawful to eat or drink, I have not erred through myself, but through these" (pointing to the chest which contained the viscera). The removal of the organs identified as the seat of the appetites was considered equivalent to the purification of the body from their evil influences.

So literally did the early Christians interpret their Scriptures that they preserved the bodies of their dead by pickling them in salt water, so that on the day of resurrection the spirit of the dead might reenter a complete and perfectly preserved body. Believing that the incisions necessary to the embalming process and the removal of the internal organs would prevent the return of the spirit to its body, the Christians buried their dead without resorting to the more elaborate mummification methods employed by the Egyptian morticians.

OSIRIS, KING OF THE UNDERWORLD[5]

---

[5] Osiris is often represented with the lower par, of his body enclosed in a mummy case or wrapped about with funeral bandages. Man's spirit consists of three distinct parts, only one of which incarnates in physical form. The human body was considered to be a tomb or sepulcher of this incarnating spirit. Therefore Osiris, a symbol of the incarnating ego, was represented with the lower half of his body mummified to indicate that he was the living spirit of man enclosed within the material form symbolized by the mummy case.

There is a romance between the active principle of God and the passive principle of Nature. From the union of these two principles is produced the rational creation. Man is a composite creature. From his Father (the active principle) he inherits his Divine Spirit, the fire of aspiration--that immortal part of himself which rises triumphant from the broken clay of mortality: that part which remains after the natural organisms have disintegrated or have been regenerated. From his Mother (the passive principle) he inherits his body--that part over which the laws of Nature have control: his humanity, his mortal personality, his appetites, his feelings, and his emotions. The Egyptians also believed that Osiris was the river Nile and that Isis

In her work on *Egyptian Magic*, Florence Farr hazards the following speculation concerning the esoteric purposes behind the practice of mummification. "There is every reason to suppose," she says, "that only those who had received some grade of initiation were mummified; for it is certain that, in the eyes of the Egyptians, mummification effectually prevented reincarnation. Reincarnation was necessary to imperfect souls, to those who had failed to pass the tests of initiation; but for those who had the Will and the capacity to enter the Secret Adytum, there was seldom necessity for that liberation of the soul which is said to be effected by the destruction of the body. The body of the Initiate was therefore preserved after death as a species of Talisman or material basis for the manifestation of the Soul upon earth."

During the period of its inception mummification was limited to the Pharaoh and such other persons of royal rank as presumably partook of the attributes of the great Osiris, the divine, mummified King of the Egyptian Underworld.

---

(his sister-wife) was the contiguous land, which, when inundated by the river, bore fruit and harvest. The murky water of the Nile were believed to account for the blackness of Osiris, who was generally symbolized as being of ebony hue.

# PART III:
# The Universal Deity

The adoration of the sun was one of the earliest and most natural forms of religious expression. Complex modern theologies are merely involvements and amplifications of this simple aboriginal belief. The primitive mind, recognizing the beneficent power of the solar orb, adored it as the proxy of the Supreme Deity. Concerning the origin of sun worship, Albert Pike makes the following concise statement in his *Morals and Dogma*: "To them [aboriginal peoples] he [the sun] was the innate fire of bodies, the fire of Nature. Author of Life, heat, and ignition, he was to them the efficient cause of all generation, for without him there was no movement, no existence, no form. He was to them immense, indivisible, imperishable, and everywhere present. It was their need of light, and of his creative energy, that was felt by all men; and nothing was more fearful to them than his absence. His beneficent influences caused his identification with the Principle of Good; and the BRAHMA of the Hindus, and MITHRAS of the Persians, and ATHOM, AMUN, PHTHA, and OSIRIS, of the Egyptians, the BEL of the Chaldeans, the ADONAI of the Phœnicians, the ADONIS and APOLLO of the Greeks, became but personifications of the Sun, the regenerating Principle, image of that fecundity which perpetuates and rejuvenates the world's existence."

Among all the nations of antiquity, altars, mounds, and temples were dedicated to the worship of the orb of day. The ruins of these sacred places yet remain, notable among them being the pyramids of Yucatan and Egypt, the snake mounds of the American Indians, the Zikkurats of Babylon and Chaldea, the round towers of Ireland, and the massive rings of uncut stone in Britain and Normandy. The Tower of Babel, which, according to the Scriptures, was built so that man might reach up to God, was probably an astronomical observatory.

Many early priests and prophets, both pagan and Christian, were versed in astronomy and astrology; their writings are best understood when read in the light of these ancient sciences. With the growth of man's knowledge of the constitution and periodicity of the heavenly bodies, astronomical principles and terminology were introduced into his religious systems. The tutelary gods were given planetary thrones, the celestial bodies being named after the deities assigned to them. The fixed stars were divided into constellations, and through these constellations wandered the sun and its planets, the latter with their accompanying satellites.

# PART IV:
# The Solar Trinity

The sun, as supreme among the celestial bodies visible to the astronomers of antiquity, was assigned to the highest of the gods and became symbolic of the supreme authority of the Creator Himself. From a deep philosophic consideration of the powers and principles of the sun has come the concept of the Trinity as it is understood in the world today. The tenet of a Triune Divinity is not peculiar to Christian or Mosaic theology, but forms a conspicuous part of the dogma of the greatest religions of both ancient and modern times. The Persians, Hindus, Babylonians, and Egyptians had their Trinities. In every instance these represented the threefold form of one Supreme Intelligence. In modern Masonry, the Deity is symbolized by an equilateral triangle, its three sides representing the primary manifestations of the Eternal One who is Himself represented as a tiny flame, called by the Hebrews *Yod*. Jakob Böhme, the Teutonic mystic, calls the Trinity *The Three Witnesses*, by means of which the Invisible is made known to the visible, tangible universe.

The origin of the Trinity is obvious to anyone who will observe the daily manifestations of the sun. This orb, being the symbol of all Light, has three distinct phases: rising, midday, and setting. The philosophers therefore divided the life of all things into three distinct parts: growth, maturity, and decay. Between the twilight of dawn and the twilight of evening is the high noon of resplendent glory. God the Father, the Creator of the world, is symbolized by the dawn. His color is blue, because the sun rising in the morning is veiled in blue mist. God the Son, the Illuminating One sent to bear witness of His Father before all the worlds, is the celestial globe at noonday, radiant and magnificent, the maned Lion of Judah, the Golden-haired Savior of the World. Yellow is His color and His power is without end. God the Holy Ghost is the sunset phase, when the orb of day, robed in flaming red, rests for a moment upon the horizon line and then vanishes into the darkness of the night to wandering the lower worlds and later rise again triumphant from the embrace of darkness.

To the Egyptians the sun was the symbol of immortality, for, while it died each night, it rose again with each ensuing dawn. Not only has the sun this diurnal activity, but it also has its annual pilgrimage, during which time it passes successively through the twelve celestial houses of the heavens, remaining in each for thirty days. Added to these it has a third path of travel, which is called the *precession of the equinoxes*, in which it retrogrades around the zodiac through the twelve signs at the rate of one degree every seventy-two years.

Concerning the annual passage of the sun through the twelve houses of the heavens, Masonic author Robert Hewitt Brown, makes the following statement: "The Sun, as he pursued his way among these 'living creatures' of the zodiac, was said, in allegorical language, either to assume the nature of or to triumph over the sign he entered. The sun thus became a Bull in Taurus, and was worshipped as such by the Egyptians under the name of Apis, and by the Assyrians as Bel, Baal, or Bul. In Leo the sun became a Lion-slayer, Hercules, and an Archer in Sagittarius. In Pisces, the Fishes, he was a fish--Dagon, or Vishnu, the fish-god of the Philistines and Hindoos."

A careful analysis of the religious systems of pagandom uncovers much evidence of the fact that its priests served the solar energy and that their Supreme Deity was in every case this Divine Light personified. Godfrey Higgins, after thirty years of inquiry into the origin of religious beliefs, is of the opinion that "All the Gods of antiquity resolved themselves into the solar fire, sometimes itself as God, or sometimes an emblem or shekinah of that higher principle, known by the name of the creative Being or God."

The Egyptian priests in many of their ceremonies wore the skins of lions, which were symbols of the solar orb, owing to the fact that the sun is exalted, dignified, and most fortunately placed in the constellation of Leo, which he rules and which was at one time the keystone of the celestial arch. Again, Hercules is the Solar Deity, for as this mighty hunter performed his twelve labors, so the sun, in traversing the twelve houses of the zodiacal band, performs during his pilgrimage twelve essential and

SOL oriens in dorso LEONIS
THE LION OF THE SUN[6]

benevolent labors for the human race and for Nature in general, Hercules, like the Egyptian priests, wore the skin of a lion for a girdle. Samson, the

---

[6] From *Maurice's Indian Antiquities*.

The sun rising over the back of the lion or, astrologically, in the back of the lion, has always been considered symbolic of power and rulership. A symbol very similar to the one above appears on the flag of Persia, whose people have always been sun worshipers. Kings and emperors have frequently associated their terrestrial power with the celestial Power of the solar orb, and have accepted the sun, or one of its symbolic beasts or birds, as their emblem. Witness the lion of the Great Mogul and the eagles of Cæsar and Napoleon.

Hebrew hero, as his name implies, is also a solar deity. His fight with the Nubian lion, his battles with the Philistines, who represent the Powers of Darkness, and his memorable feat of carrying off the gates of Gaza, all refer to aspects of solar activity. Many of the ancient peoples had more than one solar deity; in fact, all of the gods and goddesses were supposed to partake, in part at least, of the sun's effulgence.

THE WINGED GLOBE OF EGYPT[7]

The golden ornaments used by the priestcraft of the various world religions are again a subtle reference to the solar energy, as are also the crowns of kings. In ancient times, crowns had a number of points extending outward like the rays of the sun, but modern conventionalism has, in many cases, either removed the points or else bent them inward, gathered them together, and placed an orb or cross upon the point where they meet. Many of the ancient prophets, philosophers, and dignitaries carried a scepter, the upper end of which bore a representation of the solar globe surrounded by emanating rays. All the kingdoms of earth were but copies of the kingdoms of Heaven, and the kingdoms of Heaven were best symbolized by the solar kingdom, in which the sun was the supreme ruler, the planets his privy council, and all Nature the subjects of his empire.

Many deities have been associated with the sun. The Greeks believed that Apollo, Bacchus, Dionysos, Sabazius, Hercules, Jason, Ulysses, Zeus, Uranus, and Vulcan partook of either the visible or invisible attributes of the sun. The Norwegians regarded Balder the Beautiful as a solar deity,

---

[7] From *Maurice's Indian Antiquities*.

This symbol, which appears over the Pylons or gates of many Egyptian palaces and temples, is emblematic of the three persons of the Egyptian Trinity. The wings, the serpents, and the solar orb are the insignia of Ammon, Ra, and Osiris.

and Odin is often connected with the celestial orb, especially because of his one eye. Among the Egyptians, Osiris, Ra, Anubis, Hermes, and even the mysterious Ammon himself had points of resemblance with the solar disc. Isis was the mother of the sun, and even Typhon, the Destroyer, was supposed to be a form of solar energy. The Egyptian sun myth finally centered around the person of a mysterious deity called *Serapis*. The two Central American deities, *Tezcatlipoca* and *Quetzalcoatl*, while often associated with the winds, were also undoubtedly solar gods.

In Masonry the sun has many symbols. One expression of the solar energy is Solomon, whose name SOL-OM-ON is the name for the Supreme Light in three different languages. Hiram Abiff, the Hiram of the Chaldees, is also a solar deity, and the story of his attack and murder by the Ruffians, with its solar interpretation, will be found in the chapter *The Hiramic Legend*. A striking example of the important part which the sun plays in the symbols and rituals of Freemasonry is given by George Oliver, in his *Dictionary of Symbolical Masonry*, as follows:

"The sun rises in the east, and in the east is the place for the Worshipful Master. As the sun is the source of all light and warmth, so should the Worshipful Master enliven and warm the brethren to their work. Among the ancient Egyptians the sun was the symbol of divine providence." The hierophants of the Mysteries were adorned with many insignia emblematic of solar power. The sunbursts of gilt embroidery on the back of the vestments of the Catholic priesthood signify that the priest is also an emissary and representative of *Sol Invictus*.

# PART V:
# Christianity and the Sun

For reasons which they doubtless considered sufficient, those who chronicled the life and acts of Jesus found it advisable to metamorphose him into a solar deity. The historical Jesus was forgotten; nearly all the salient incidents recorded in the four Gospels have their correlations in the movements, phases, or functions of the heavenly bodies.

Among other allegories borrowed by Christianity from pagan antiquity is the story of the beautiful, blue-eyed Sun God, with His golden hair falling upon His shoulders, robed from head to foot in spotless white and carrying in His arms the Lamb of God, symbolic of the vernal equinox. This handsome youth is a composite of Apollo, Osiris, Orpheus, Mithras, and Bacchus, for He has certain characteristics in common with each of these pagan deities.

The philosophers of Greece and Egypt divided the life of the sun during the year into four parts; therefore, they symbolized the Solar Man by four different figures. When He was born in the winter solstice, the Sun God was symbolized as a dependent infant who in some mysterious manner had managed to escape the Powers of Darkness seeking to destroy Him while He was still in the cradle of winter. The sun, being weak at this season of the year, had no golden rays (or locks of hair), but the survival of the light through the darkness of winter was symbolized by one tiny hair which alone adorned the head of the Celestial Child (as the birth of the sun took place in Capricorn, it was often represented as being suckled by a goat).

At the vernal equinox, the sun had grown to be a beautiful youth. His golden hair hung in ringlets on his shoulders and his light, as Schiller said, extended to all parts of infinity. At the summer solstice, the sun became a strong man, heavily bearded, who, in the prime of maturity, symbolized the fact that Nature at this period of the year is strongest and most fecund. At the autumnal equinox, the sun was pictured as an aged man, shuffling along with bended back and whitened locks into the oblivion of winter darkness. Thus, twelve months were assigned to the sun as the length of its life. During this period, it circled the twelve signs of the zodiac in a magnificent triumphal march. When fall came, it entered, like Samson, into the house of Delilah (Virgo), where its rays were cut off and it lost its strength. In Masonry, the cruel winter months are symbolized by three murderers who sought to destroy the God of Light and Truth.

The coming of the sun was hailed with joy; the time of its departure was viewed as a period to be set aside for sorrow and unhappiness. This glorious, radiant orb of day, the true light "which lighteth every man who cometh into the world," the supreme benefactor, who raised all things from the dead, who fed the hungry multitudes, who stilled the tempest, who after dying rose again and restored all things to life--this Supreme Spirit of humanitarianism and philanthropy is known to Christendom as Christ, the Redeemer of worlds, the Only Begotten of The Father, the Word made Flesh, and the Hope of Glory.

# PART VI:
# The Birthday of the Sun

The pagans set aside the 25th of December as the birthday of the Solar Man. They rejoiced, feasted, gathered in processions, and made offerings in the temples. The darkness of winter was over and the glorious son of light was returning to the Northern Hemisphere. With his last effort the old Sun God had torn down the house of the Philistines (*the Spirits of Darkness*) and had cleared the way for the new sun who was born that day from the depths of the earth amidst the symbolic beasts of the lower world.

THE THREE SUNS[8]

---

[8] From Lilly's *Astrological Predictions for 1648, 1649, and 1650*.)

The following description of this phenomenon appears in a letter written by Jeremiah Shakerley in Lancashire, March 4th, 1648:--"On Monday the 28th of February last, there arose with the Sun two Parelii, on either side one; their distance from him was by estimation, about ten degrees; they continued still of the same distance from the Zenith, or height above the Horizon, that the Sun did; and from the parts averse to the Sun, there seemed to issue out certain bright rays, not unlike those which the Sun sendeth from behind a cloud, but brighter. The parts of these Parelii which were toward the Sun, were of a mixt colour, wherein green and red were most predominant. A little above them was a thin rainbow, scarcely discernible, of a bright colour, with the concave towards the Sun, and the ends thereof seeming to touch the Parelii: Above that, in a clear diaphanous ayr, [air], appeared another conspicuous Rainbow, beautified with divers colours; it was as neer as I could discern to the Zenith; it seemed of something a lesser radius than the other, they being back to back, yet a pretty way between. At or neer the apparent

Concerning this season of celebration, an anonymous Master of Arts of Balliol College, Oxford, in his scholarly treatise, *Mankind Their Origin and Destiny*, says:

> "The Romans also had their solar festival, and their games of the circus in honor of the birth of the god of day. It took place the eighth day before the kalends of January--that is, on December 25. Servius, in his commentary on verse 720 of the seventh book of the Æneid, in which Virgil speaks of the new sun, says that, properly speaking, the sun is new on the 8th of the Kalends of January-that is, December 25. In the time of Leo I., some of the Fathers of the Church said that "what rendered the festival (*of Christmas*) venerable was less the birth of Jesus Christ than the return, and, as they expressed it, the new birth of the sun." It was on the same day that the birth of the Invincible Sun (*Natalis Solis Invicti*), was celebrated at Rome, as can be seen in the Roman calendars, published in the reign of Constantine and of Julian. This epithet 'Invictus' is the same as the Persians gave to this same god, whom they worshipped by the name of Mithra, and whom they caused to be born in a grotto, just as he is represented as being born in a stable, under the name of Christ, by the Christians."

Concerning the Catholic Feast of the Assumption and its parallel in astronomy, the same author adds:

> "At the end of eight months, when the sun-god, having increased, traverses the eighth sign, he absorbs the celestial Virgin in his fiery course, and she disappears in the midst of the luminous rays and the glory of her son. This phenomenon, which takes place every year about the middle of August, gave rise to a festival which still exists, and in which it is supposed that the mother of Christ, laying aside her earthly life, is associated with the glory of her son, and is placed at his side in the heavens. The Roman calendar of Columella marks the death or disappearance of Virgo

---

time of the full Moon, they vanished, leaving abundance of terror and amazement in those that saw them. (See William Lilly.)

at this period. The sun, he says, passes into Virgo on the thirteenth day before the kalends of September. This is where the Catholics place the Feast of the Assumption, or the reunion of the Virgin to her Son. This feast was formerly called the feast of the Passage of the Virgin; and in the Library of the Fathers we have an account of the Passage of the Blessed Virgin. The ancient Greeks and Romans fix the assumption of Astraea, who is also this same Virgin, on that day."

This Virgin mother, giving birth to the Sun God which Christianity has so faithfully preserved, is a reminder of the inscription concerning her Egyptian prototype, Isis, which appeared on the Temple of Sais: *"The fruit which I have brought forth is the Sun."* While the Virgin was associated with the moon by the early pagans, there is no doubt that they also understood her position as a constellation in the heavens, for nearly all the peoples of antiquity credit her as being the mother of the sun, and they realized that although the moon could not occupy that position, the sign of Virgo could, and did, give birth to the sun out of her side on the 25th day of December. Albertus Magnus states, "We know that the sign of the Celestial Virgin rose over the Horizon at the moment at which we fix the birth of our Lord Jesus Christ."

Among certain of the Arabian and Persian astronomers the three stars forming the sword belt of Orion were called the Magi who came to pay homage to the young Sun God. The author of *Mankind--Their Origin and Destiny* contributes the following additional information: "In Cancer, which had risen to the meridian at midnight, is the constellation of the Stable and of the Ass. The ancients called it Præsepe Jovis. In the north the stars of the Bear are seen, called by the Arabians Martha and Mary, and also the coffin of Lazarus." Thus, the esotericism of pagandom was embodied in Christianity, although its keys are lost. The Christian church blindly follows ancient customs, and when asked for a reason gives superficial and unsatisfactory explanations, either forgetting or ignoring the indisputable fact that each religion is based upon the secret doctrines of its predecessor.

# PART VII:
# The Three Suns

The solar orb, like the nature of man, was divided by the ancient sages into three separate bodies. According to the mystics, there are three suns in each solar system, analogous to the three centers of life in each individual constitution. These are called three lights: the *spiritual* sun, the *intellectual* or *soular* sun, and the *material* sun (*now symbolized in Freemasonry by three candles*). The spiritual sun manifests the power of God the Father; the soular sun radiates the life of God the Son; and the material sun is the vehicle of manifestation for God the Holy Spirit. Man's nature was divided by the mystics into three distinct parts: spirit, soul, and body. His physical body was unfolded and vitalized by the material sun; his spiritual nature was illuminated by the spiritual sun; and his intellectual nature was redeemed by the true *light of grace*--the soular sun. The alignment of these three globes in the heavens was one explanation offered for the peculiar fact that the orbits of the planets are not circular but elliptical.

The pagan priests always considered the solar system as a *Grand Man*, and drew their analogy of these three centers of activity from the three main centers of life in the human body: the brain, the heart, and the generative system. The Transfiguration of Jesus describes three tabernacles, the largest being in the center (the heart), and a smaller one on either side (the brain and the generative system). It is possible that the philosophical hypothesis of the existence of the three suns is based upon a peculiar natural phenomenon which has occurred many times in history. In the fifty-first year after Christ three suns were seen at once in the sky and also in the sixty-sixth year. In the sixty-ninth year, two suns were seen together. According to William Lilly, between the years 1156 and 1648 twenty similar occurrences were recorded.

Recognizing the sun as the supreme benefactor of the material world, Hermetists believed that there was a spiritual sun which ministered to the needs of the invisible and divine part of Nature--human and universal Anent this subject, the great Paracelsus wrote: "There is an earthly sun, which is the cause of all heat, and all who are able to see may see the sun;

and those who are blind and cannot see him may feel his heat. There is an Eternal Sun, which is the source of all wisdom, and those whose spiritual senses have awakened to life will see that sun and be conscious of His existence; but those who have not attained spiritual consciousness may yet feel His power by an inner faculty which is called Intuition."

Certain Rosicrucian scholars have given special appellations to these three phases of the sun: the spiritual sun they called *Vulcan*; the soular and intellectual sun, Christ and Lucifer respectively; and the material sun, the Jewish Demiurgus *Jehovah*. Lucifer here represents the intellectual mind without the illumination of the spiritual mind; therefore, it is "the false light." The false light is finally overcome and redeemed by the true light of the soul, called the *Second Logos* or *Christ*. The secret processes by which the Luciferian intellect is transmuted into the Christly intellect constitute one of the great secrets of alchemy, and are symbolized by the process of transmuting base metals into gold.

In the rare treatise *The Secret Symbols of The Rosicrucians*, Franz Hartmann defines the sun alchemically as: "The symbol of Wisdom. The Centre of Power or Heart of things. The Sun is a centre of energy and a storehouse of power. Each living being contains within itself a centre of life, which may grow to be a Sun. In the heart of the regenerated, the divine power, stimulated by the Light of the Logos, grows into a Sun which illuminates his mind." In a note, the same author amplifies his description by adding: "The terrestrial sun is the image or reflection of the invisible celestial sun; the former is in the realm of Spirit what the latter is in the realm of Matter; but the latter receives its power from the former."

In the majority of cases, the religions of antiquity agree that the material visible sun was a reflector rather than a source of power. The sun was sometimes represented as a shield carried on the arm of the Sun God, as for example, Frey, the Scandinavian Solar Deity. This sun reflected the light of the invisible *spiritual* sun, which was the true source of life, light, and truth. The physical nature of the universe is receptive; it is a realm of effects. The invisible causes of these effects belong to the spiritual world. Hence, the spiritual world is the sphere of *causation*; the material world is the sphere of *effects*; while the intellectual--or soul--world is the sphere of *mediation*. Thus Christ, the personified higher intellect and soul nature, is called "the Mediator" who, by virtue of His position and power, says: "No man cometh to the Father, but by me."

What the sun is to the solar system, the spirit is to the bodies of man; for his natures, organs, and functions are as planets surrounding the central life (or sun) and living upon its emanations. The solar power in man is divided into three parts, which are termed the threefold human spirit of man. All three of these spiritual natures are said to be radiant and transcendent; united, they form the Divinity in man. Man's threefold lower nature--consisting of his physical organism, his emotional nature, and his mental faculties--reflects the light of his threefold Divinity and bears witness of It in the physical world. Man's three bodies are symbolized by an upright triangle; his threefold spiritual nature by an inverted triangle. These two triangles, when united in the form of a six-pointed star, were called by the Jews "the Star of David," "the Signet of Solomon," and are more commonly known today as "the Star of Zion." These triangles symbolize the spiritual and material universes linked together in the constitution of the human creature, who partakes of both Nature and Divinity. Man's animal nature partakes of the earth; his divine nature of the heavens; his human nature of the mediator.

# PART VIII:
# The Celestial Inhabitants of the Sun

The Rosicrucians and the Illuminati, describing the angels, archangels, and other celestial creatures, declared that they resembled small suns, being centers of radiant energy surrounded by streamers of Vrilic force. From these outpouring streamers of force is derived the popular belief that angels have wings. These wings are corona-like fans of light, by means of which the celestial creatures propel themselves through the subtle essences of the superphysical worlds.

SURYA, THE REGENT OF THE SUN[9]

True mystics are unanimous in their denial of the theory that the angels and archangels are human in form, as so often pictured. A human

---

[9] From Moor's *Hindu Pantheon*.
Moor describes this figure as follows: "The cast is nine inches in height, representing the glorious god of day-holding the attributes of VISHNU, seated on a seven-headed serpent; his car drawn by a seven-headed horse, driven by the legless ARUN, a personification of the dawn, or AURORA." (See Moor's Hindu Pantheon.)

figure would be utterly useless in the ethereal substances through which they manifest. Science has long debated the probability of the other planets being inhabited. Objections to the idea are based upon the argument that creatures with human organisms could not possibly exist in the environments of Mars, Jupiter, Uranus, and Neptune. This argument fails to take into account Nature's universal law of adjustment to environment. The ancients asserted that life originated from the sun, and that everything when bathed in the light of the solar orb was capable of absorbing the solar life elements and later radiating them as flora and fauna. One philosophical concept regarded the sun as a parent and the planets as embryos still connected to the solar body by means of ethereal umbilical cords which served as channels to convey life and nourishment to the planets.

Some secret orders have taught that the sun was inhabited by a race of creatures with bodies composed of a radiant, spiritual ether not unlike in its constituency the actual glowing ball of the sun itself. The solar heat had no harmful effect upon them, because their organisms were sufficiently refined and sensitized to harmonize with the sun's tremendous vibratory rate. These creatures resemble miniature suns, being a little larger than a dinner plate in size, although some of the more powerful are considerably larger. Their color is the golden white light of the sun, and from them emanate four streamers of Vril. These streamers are often of great length and are in constant motion. A peculiar palpitation is to be noted throughout the structure of the globe and is communicated in the form of ripples to the emanating streamers. The greatest and most luminous of these spheres is the Archangel Michael; and the entire order of solar life, which resemble him and dwell upon the sun, are called by modern Christians "the archangels" or "the spirits of the light."

# PART IX:
# The Sun in Alchemical Symbology

Gold is the metal of the sun and has been considered by many as crystallized sunlight. When gold is mentioned in alchemical tracts, it may be either the metal itself or the celestial orb which is the source, or spirit, of gold. Sulphur because of its fiery nature was also associated with the sun.

As gold was the symbol of spirit and the base metals represented man's lower nature, certain alchemists were called "miners" and were pictured with picks and shovels digging into the earth in search of the precious metal--those finer traits of character buried in the earthiness of materiality and ignorance. The diamond concealed in the heart of the black carbon illustrated the same principle. The Illuminati used a pearl hidden in the shell of an oyster at the bottom of the sea to signify spiritual powers. Thus, the seeker after truth became a pearl-fisher: he descended into the sea of material illusion in search of understanding, termed by the initiates "the Pearl of Great Price."

When the alchemists stated that every animate and inanimate thing in the universe contained the seeds of gold, they meant that even the grains of sand possessed a spiritual nature, for gold was the spirit of all things. Concerning these seeds of spiritual gold the following Rosicrucian axiom is significant: "A seed is useless and impotent unless it is put in its appropriate matrix." Franz Hartmann, in his book *In the Pronaos of the Temple of Wisdom*, comments on this axiom with these illuminating words: "A soul cannot develop and progress without an appropriate body, because it is the physical body that furnishes the material for its development."

The purpose of alchemy was not to make something out of nothing but rather to fertilize and nurture the seed which was already present. Its processes did not actually create gold but rather made the ever-present seed of gold grow and flourish. Everything which exists has a spirit--the seed of Divinity within itself--and regeneration is not the process of attempting to place something where it previously had not existed.

Regeneration actually means the unfoldment of the omnipresent Divinity in man, that this Divinity may shine forth as a sun and illumine all with whom it comes in contact.

# PART X:
# The Midnight Sun

Apuleius said when describing his initiation: "At midnight I saw the sun shining with a splendid light." The midnight sun was also part of the mystery of alchemy. It symbolized the spirit in man shining through the darkness of his human organisms. It also referred to the spiritual sun in the solar system, which the mystic could see as well at midnight as at high noon, the material earth bring powerless to obstruct the rays of this Divine orb. The mysterious lights which illuminated the temples of the Egyptian Mysteries during the nocturnal hours were said by some to be reflections of the spiritual sun gathered by the magical powers of the priests. The weird light seen ten miles below the surface of the earth by I-AM-THE-MAN in that remarkable Masonic allegory *Etidorhpa* (Aphrodite spelt backward) may well refer to the mysterious midnight sun of the ancient rites.

Primitive conceptions concerning the warfare between the principles of Good and Evil were often based upon the alternations of day and night. During the Middle Ages, the practices of black magic were confined to the nocturnal hours; and those who served the Spirit of Evil were called black magicians, while those who served the Spirit of Good were called white magicians. Black and white were associated respectively with night and day, and the endless conflict of light and shadow is alluded to many times in the mythologies of various peoples.

The Egyptian Demon, Typhon, was symbolized as part crocodile and part hog because these animals are gross and earthy in both appearance and temperament. Since the world began, living things have feared the darkness; those few creatures who use it as a shield for their maneuvers were usually connected with the Spirit of Evil. Consequently cats, bats, toads, and owls are associated with witchcraft. In certain parts of Europe, it is still believed that at night black magicians assume the bodies of wolves and roam around destroying. From this notion originated the stories of the werewolves. Serpents, because they lived in the earth, were associated with the Spirit of Darkness. As the battle between Good and Evil centers around the use of the generative forces of Nature, winged serpents represent the regeneration of the animal nature of man or those Great Ones in whom this regeneration is complete. Among the Egyptians the sun's rays are often shown ending in human hands. Masons will find a connection between these hands and the well-known *Paw of the Lion* which raises all things to life with its grip.

# PART XI:
# Solar Colors

The theory so long held of three primary and four secondary colors is purely exoteric, for since the earliest periods it has been known that there are seven, and not three, primary colors, the human eye being capable of estimating only three of them. Thus, although green can be made by combining blue and yellow, there is also a true or primary green which is not a compound. This can he proved by breaking up the spectrum with a prism. Helmholtz found that the so-called secondary colors of the spectrum could not be broken up into their supposed primary colors. Thus, the orange of the spectrum, if passed through a second prism, does not break up into red and yellow but remains orange.

Consciousness, intelligence, and force are fittingly symbolized by the colors blue, yellow, and red. The therapeutic effects of the colors, moreover, are in harmony with this concept, for blue is a fine, soothing, electrical color; yellow, a vitalizing and refining color; and red, an agitating and heat-giving color. It has also been demonstrated that minerals and plants affect the human constitution according to their colors. Thus, a yellow flower generally yields a medicine that affects the constitution in a manner similar to yellow light or the musical tone *mi*. An orange flower will influence in a manner similar to orange light and, being one of the so-called secondary colors, corresponds either to the tone *re* or to the chord of *do* and *mi*.

The ancients conceived the spirit of man to correspond with the color blue, the mind with yellow, and the body with red. Heaven is therefore blue, earth yellow, and hell--or the underworld--red. The fiery condition of the inferno merely symbolizes the nature of the sphere or plane of force of which it is composed. In the Greek Mysteries the irrational sphere was always considered as red, for it represented that condition in which the consciousness is enslaved by the lusts and passions of the lower nature. In India certain of the gods--usually attributes of Vishnu--are depicted with blue skin to signify their divine and supermundane constitution. According to esoteric philosophy, blue is the true and sacred color of the sun. The apparent orange-yellow shade of this orb is the result of its rays being immersed in the substances of the illusionary world.

THE SOLAR FACE[10]

In the original symbolism of the Christian Church, colors were of first importance and their use was regulated according to carefully prepared rules. Since the Middle Ages, however, the carelessness with which colors have been employed has resulted in the loss of their deeper emblematic meanings. In its primary aspect, white or silver signified life, purity, innocence, joy, and light; red, the suffering and death of Christ and His saints, and also divine love, blood, and warfare or suffering; blue, the heavenly sphere and the states of godliness and contemplation; yellow or gold, glory, fruitfulness, and goodness; green, fecundity, youthfulness, and prosperity; violet, humility, deep affection, and sorrow; black, death, destruction, and humiliation. In early church art the colors of robes and

---

[10] From Montfaucon's *Antiquities*.

The corona of the sun is here shown in the form of a lion's mane. This is a subtle reminder of the fact that at one time the summer solstice took place in the sign of Leo, the Celestial Lion.

ornaments also revealed whether a saint had been martyred, as well as the character of the work that he had done to deserve canonization.

In addition to the colors of the spectrum there are a vast number of vibratory color waves, some too low and others too high to be registered by the human optical apparatus. It is appalling to contemplate man's colossal ignorance concerning these vistas of abstract space.

As in the past man explored unknown continents, so in the future, armed with curious implements fashioned for the purpose, he will explore these little known fastnesses of light, color, sound, and consciousness.

www.ingramcontent.com/pod-product-compliance
Lightning Source LLC
LaVergne TN
LVHW041500070426
835507LV00009B/719